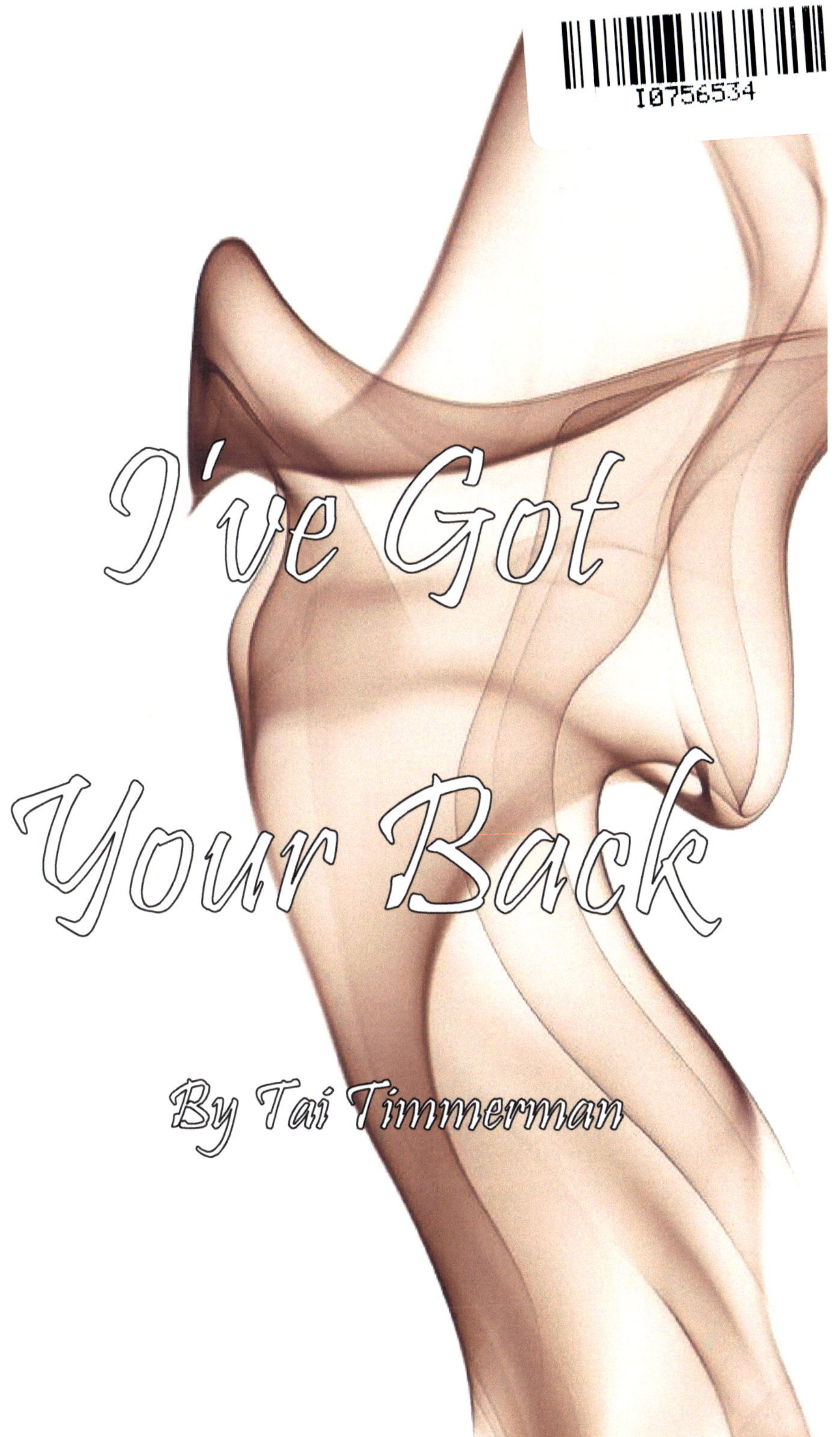
I'0756534
I've Got
Your Back
By Tai Timmerman

Published by Barnes & Noble Publishers

Cover design by Barnes & Noble Publishers

ISBN: Printed in the United States

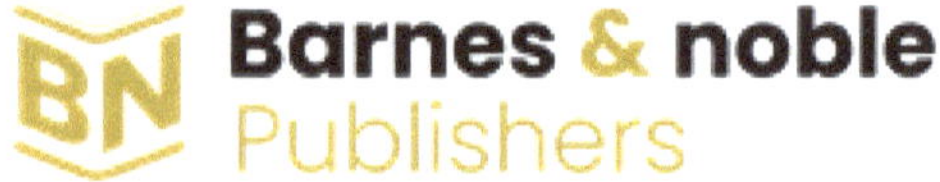

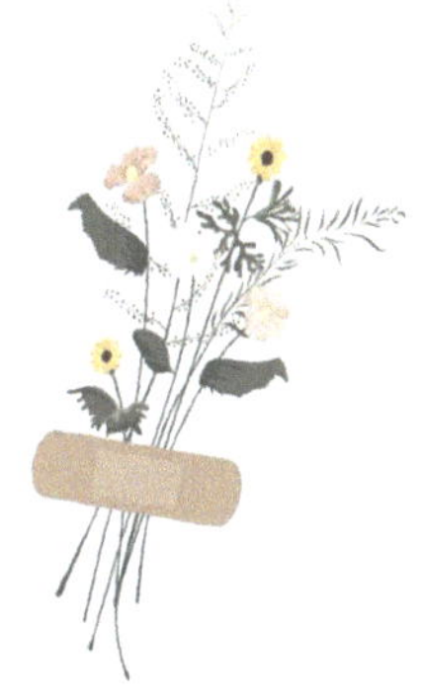

Dedication

To all of those struggling with their mental health

Acknowledgments

Special thanks to Glenn Joseph from Barnes and Noble Publishers for believing in my vision. This continuing dream of mine would not have been possible without the entire Barnes and Noble Publisher's Company.

I would also like to thank my friends and family for their support, especially my friends at Howard University. Lastly, I would like to thank everybody who purchased this book.

Preface

"Mental health...is not a destination, but a process. It's about how you drive, not where you're going."

—Noam Shpancer, Ph.D

TABLE OF CONTENTS

Introduction: A Cry For Help

A cry for help—silent croon, ravens and eagles hover over me.

A cry for mercy— tears across a lagoon, Angels and Heavens attempt to set me free.

Hidden in a dark room with flowers waiting for my strength to bloom.

Show me the light when times are tough.

Give me some time, And I'll be home... *Soon.*

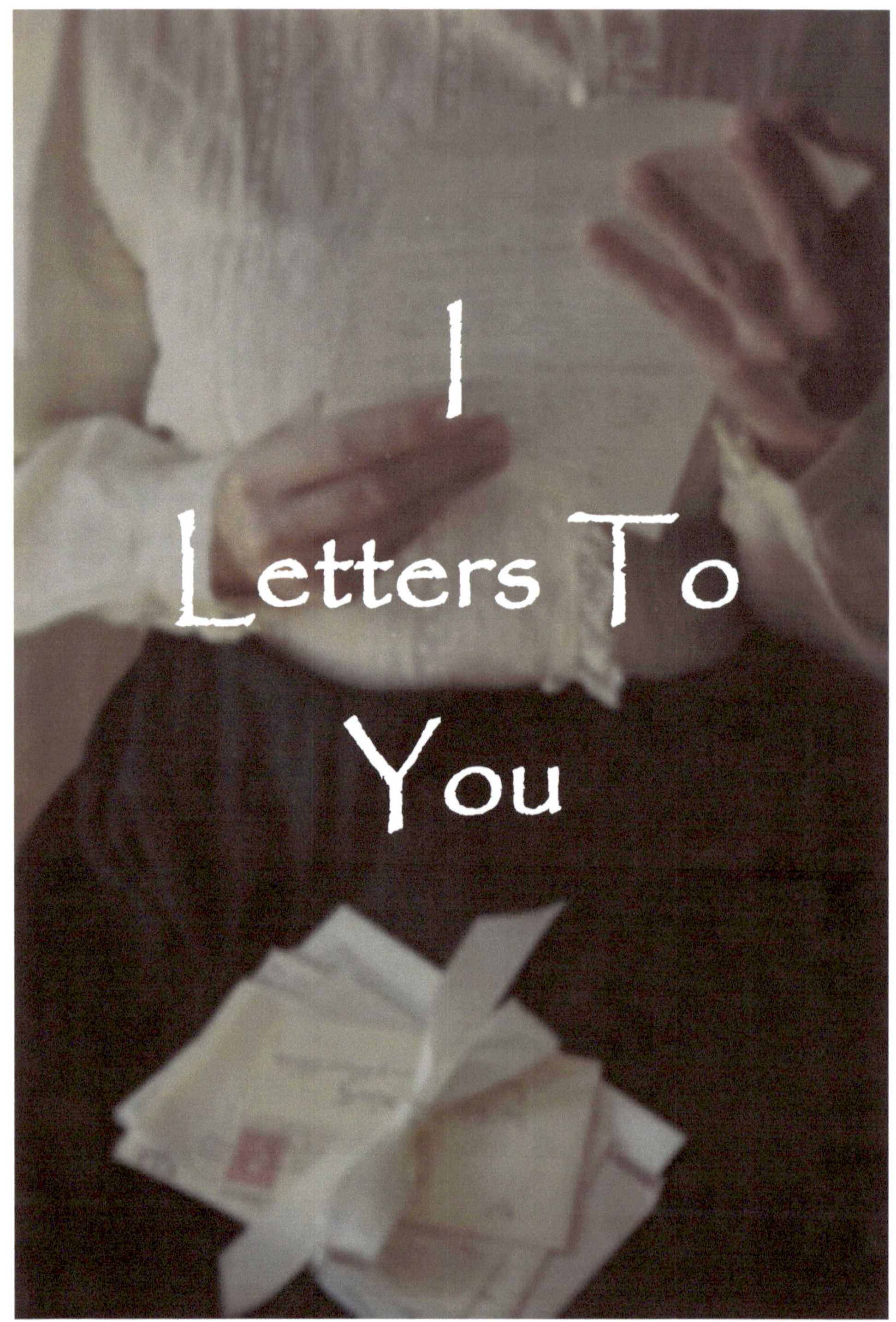
I
Letters To
You

Angry

Dear Mr. Anger,

Please Leave Me Alone.

I Do Not Like Suffering In Silence.

Listen To The Infernos You've Caused Like Lucifer
As The Bone-Chilling Tears Liberate You To Your
So-Called Freedom.

Explosive And Aggressive

More Than Dynamite,

It Is Hard To Contain Like A Volcanic Eruption.

Best Regards,

An Adult trying to navigate the world

Written on Her Sleeve

Tattoos as a form

Of Expression And Art

Sketched All Over Her Body In The Light,

While Her Scars

Were Etched All Over Her Arms In The Dark.

Too Close To Comfort

It Was Too Late To Ask For ***Help..***

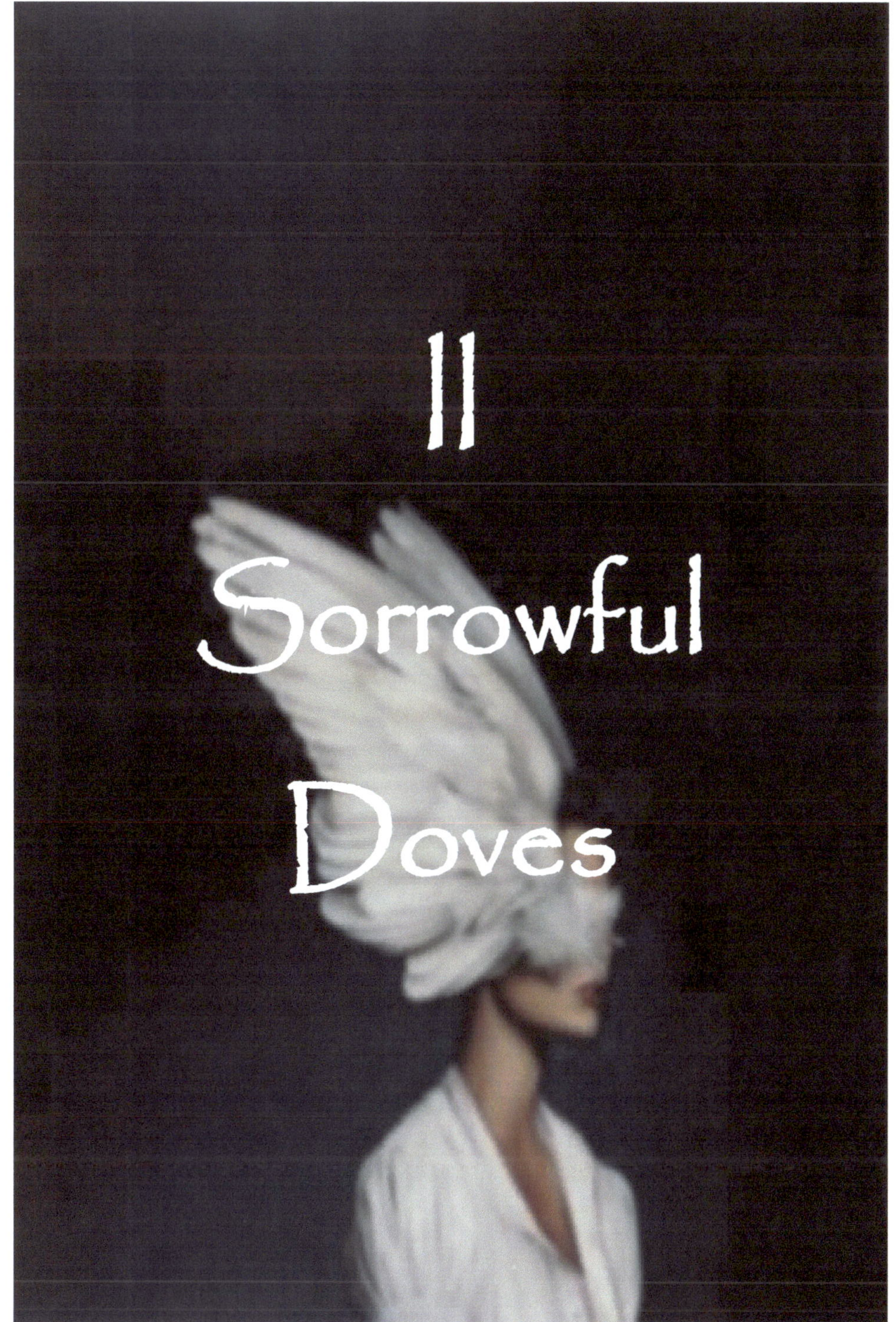
II
Sorrowful
Doves

Desolate

A cage without doors or metal bars—sentencing your thoughts for life.

The shadows of disarray appear in the moonlight with your scars etched in the Big Dipper for all to see.

An ocean of emptiness where Phanes meets Thanatos below a flame tree.

As you lay your head to rest upon the cornerstone of isolation, its slender fingers and macabre eyes pierce through the sorrows of common passions.

What's passion without fire?

What's fire without oxygen?

What's oxygen without...?

Life?...

To breathe in fog, while clouds as dark as obsidian seem to prey over to attack at night.

Hidden Scars

Invisible To The Naked Eye So That No One Could See.

I Am Living In Spain.

And Just Minusing The "S" Daily... Wondering If I'll Ever Know How Serenity Truly Feels.

My Smile Hides The Thousand Unseen Scars Like A Bandit

In The Caliginous Night...

As The Moon Scampers Away From The Stars.

Help Me

To Forget My Odious Past

The Kind Touch...

Towards The Back Of My Ear Lobe.

Help Me

To Learn To Love Again Like A Child Learning How To Ride A Bike.

The Cuts And Bruises That Life Caused—It Caused Me To Push Everyone Away.

And Caused Me To Have A Black Pit In My Stomach—Emptiness Tears Stuck My Eyelids Together Like Candle Wax.

Wear A Happy-Go-Lucky Mask Just To Come Home And Take It Off.

Put My Feelings Inside Of A Box So I Can Think Outside It.

Invisible To The Naked Eyes So That No One Could See.

'Read from the bottom to the top as well!'

Melancholy

Gloomiest Of Ghosts,

As A Grim Reaper Walks To Me

And Hands Me A Glass Of Spirits In An Attempt

To Make Me Feel Warm On The Inside.

Sadness Beyond Measure

When The Perpendicular Equation Is Equaling Sin ϴ+2π.

Signing Off On A Goldenrod Piece Of Paper With My Sins Involved.

Depression Is The Filling

Of The Wheat Crust In A Pie

And Eating It Leads To My Gluttony Downfall;

We Love The Fall When It's Blush Red, Cyber Yellow, And Chartreuse Green Leaves Step

Into The Wind On A Tree

Until Death Does Them Part....

Ceremony of Pain

A Thread Of Blood And

A Tsunami Woven Into Your Heart,

Concealed Words—Lethal

As Weapons Jagged Around Your

Fists Like The Feathers Of A Forest Raven.

Invisible To The Moon And Eyes,

Invisible To Your Subconscious,

Sutures With Pain, As It Pulls You Down.

Tangled Around Your Thoughts,

Tied To Your Everlasting Nightmares Of Life.

Losing Your Mind

Want to escape misery through your company in a world that's black and white. Every time you attempt to paint a colorful landscape in its beauty, your paintbrush transfigures your happiness into woefulness. Ploddingly laying your art supplies on the table because you are nowhere to be found...

Nowhere.

III

Addictions

Broken Moments

In anticipation, the atmosphere holds its breath,

A shattered antique record spins, dancing with death.

Fragments of bones run, the skin becomes bruised,

He wobbles down to his seat, battered and bemused.

He asks the waitress for a drink so that he can forget his mind's poignancy— the physical pain of unfulfilled promises.

He committed to saving his money in the bank, yet he trusted the bar more.

One shot, two shots, three shots...

Again and

Again and

Again

With each taste of Whiskey, he gets a warm attachment to the antediluvian record player of sadness on his doorstep— the rhythm and blues of life.

Slow Inhales

Hiss hiss is the noise a lighter makes as it kisses lips with a cigarette.

Smoke batters and swings in the air.

Can you feel the nicotine rush in your lungs?

Feel the urge to breathe in loneliness.

Little do you know, crinkling paper burns tobacco's ashes through your lack of boundaries.

The Parade

I hear the children's screams, reaching for mommies and daddies,

Longing for one more embrace in their innocent lullabies.

As I unlatch the emergency exit, a city parade comes into view,

Where wilted flowers on sidewalks, signed by prescription drugs, they rue.

All I remember are the sirens of ambulances scripting names of loved one's names in the sky...

With purple-colored paint—

Circular Ivory colored pills drift into the cracks of the fake picket fences.

America was made to believe.

It's hard to fight for a cause when clinics are prescribing inked poppy plant petals to relieve—

Years of generational curses saying,

"Refill, refill, refill!

Can we please have a refill?"

But honestly, can I go back to seeing a parade inside my city, where kids are not witnessing wilted flowers on sidewalks, autographing prescription drugs?

Winners Lose By Fate

You're in it to win it at a price to pay

In the end, for all of your losses.

Interlude: The Phone Call Upstairs...

Ring ring ring

Ring ring ring...

The telephone leap frog hopped off of the desk, as he stares into his darkest secrets with a mirror.

Shaped in blue signed a note to the Grim Reaper—a contractual agreement.

Heard the message of agony and decided to accept the phone call upstairs.

IV

Perfectly Strange

Panic Attack

Your chest slowly caves in with a spindle of intensity, as it rises and falls to the pit of your stomach.

The walls slam the door shut out of rage—hyperventilating sleepy hallows follow the race between your Heart and mind.

Yes, it was a bad dream.

A very, very bad dream. You hope to never dream about venturous experiences.

Your world is a kaleidoscope of darkness in a tunnel.

Where everything is out of your control.

The Love Song of Jazz

He Played Those Old Weary Blues, As The Saxophone Blazed Autumnal Tunes—Wearing His Sharp Navy Blue Suit And Golden Cuff Links On, The Streets Of East 125th, Lifting Spirits With A Glass Of Compassion In Their Hands.

Swaying To The Sun.

Swaying To The Moon.

A Voice, Smooth As Butterscotch, Serenade The Hearts Of People—Stopped To Stare At A Beautiful Personification—Raw Talent.

All Of A Sudden Dissonance Protrudes The
Street And The Souls.

Nervousness Followed By A Count Of The
Trombone Spewing Shortness Of Breath

Violins Scream *Accelerato* While The Jazz Bass
Has Difficulty Resting In Between Chords.

Disharmony In The Sun

Disharmony In The Moon

Fear

Is Fear, The Despised Four-Letter Foe, Anxiety's
Speed Chase, Dreams It Does Overthrow.

On Belt Parkway, 130 Miles An Hour It Takes
Flight, Cooking Us Up In The Kitchen Of Fright.

Like Grandma On A Frivolous Friday Morn,

It Grabs A Plate From Our Self-Conscious Mind,

All Forlorn.

Devouring Our Peace, It Feasts Without Care,
Leaving Us Vulnerable, Caught In Its Snare.

Threats And Triggers, You, A Provocateur,
Unleashing Knuckles Or Prompting Flights To
Soar.

Beware The Line, Above Or Below The Belt, As I
Ignite A Lighter, Fears Must Be Dealt.

In The Box Challenge, Cautiously Tread, Respect
Your Boundaries, For Anyone, Don't Be Mislead.

Embrace Your True Self, Let It Shine, Fear, A Four-Letter Word, Holds Insignificance In This Design.

The fear is a four-letter word with little to no **significance.**

Weather Forecast

Clouds Catapult,

Voluminous And Stygian Braiding Obliteration Through Your Windowpane.

Thunder And Lightning Strike Through Your Delicate Soul— Through The Cast-Iron Ground— Through The Dense Earth.

Suffocating In A Chamber Of Letters...

Numbers... Words... Thoughts...

Pretty Brown Eyes Illuminate A Reflection— Shooting Stars Of Worry And Doubt.

The Temptation To Self-Soothe In The Rain,

While The Tears Shed Are Overflowing Into The Great Pond, Then The Volta River, And Finally Within The Pacific Ocean.

Sobbing Until No One Can Hear Your Cries. All You Hear Is A Gasp For Air, As The Wind Takes Hold Of Your Dread—The Hurricanes Pursue Your Restlessness With Palm Trees Ruffling Your Nervousness.

Oh...

I Am Wondering Where The Wondrous Rainbows, With Cotton Candy-Like Clouds Are.

Put Their Mind At Ease Instead Of The Raindrops Of Anxiety.

V
PTSD

War

Build me up to break me down in never-ending curses already replaying in my head.

Nightmares

Dull and hallow

Screaming for it to go away

The person I once knew...

Gone

Storms of hurricanes

Stung me like a bee

Have been destroyed

Concentrated rage of the fire

Slaughter tears in the clouds

VI
Self-care

Fall

Frolicking in the Sandstone Orange and Canary Yellow leaves.

As I sip my balmy Chamomile tea into new horizons.

Lying on the luscious grass, while eating an Apple Cider donut in the vibrant blue sky.

Laugh like there's no tomorrow.

Summer

Sleeping in while the television is on, grandma is cooking in the kitchen, and I dream about the driving force of my reality.

Under the sea where I befriended a Hector Dolphin and she taught me about mindfulness.

Memories I create with my lovable friends.

Madness of nature's call—forest destruction

Every beach bore the fruits of my emotional traumas.

Racing through Coney Island Boardwalk to eat flowered-shaped mangos.

Beaches and Palm Trees

Calm waves snuggle the omnipresent palm trees.

Sonnets in the sunlight profess their self-love to the Turquoise Blue skies.

As the little boy was learning how to swim, the voice of the ocean embraced the paroxysmal tides that controlled its Mars.

Together, he and his father built a sand castle to scrape the stars.

"Oh, how fun it is to love Nature when it loves you back," exclaimed the little boy.

"You should not love Nature because it loves you back. You should love Nature because you love yourself, " said the father.

Shadow Work

Forgive yourself for not knowing your boundaries.

Forgive yourself for reopening wounds.

Always forgive yourself.

Stretch and Take My Hand

Don't Quit. Breathe In And Breathe Out.

Tune Out All Of The Noise And Focus On Me And How Your Body.

Is Supposed To Feel In The Present Moment.

Treat Your Body As A Temple— With Kindness. Step Into The Unknown As Stretching Provides A Path Of Health And Abundance.

Take My Hand And Reach.

Out And Trust Your Intuition about the ego and tamed.

Plant Parent

Garden Grounds Gallant Gaillardia, Green Gallium, Glorious Gloriosa Grandiloquently.

Water-Waken Wildflowers Wait Warmly With Wandering Walks Welcomingly. Sing Psalms Stunningly So The Skies Scream.

Touch My Feet With Grace And Empathy With Vines Violent As The Sea, Yet Calmly Speaks To Me.

Cups of Tea with Grandma and Grandpa

The living room is filled with fragrant scents.

Behind me is the crystalline China Cabinets with golden herbs.

Black and green leaves curl against tulip petals and lavender until they feel reassurance.

My grandparents sit with me at the dining room table with carnation milk throughout the air to sip away stressful days.

VII

Purposeful Intervention

You Matter

There are thousands of gardens inside of you
waiting to be nurtured by your talents—

Thousands of people that want to love your
insecurities as their security from the wild.
Forever significant to others.

You matter!

Your Awakening

Close your eyes.

Now open them.

What do you see?

Do you see darkness?

Your answer is wrong.

Close your eyes.

Now open them.

What do you see now?

Do you see lightness?

Your answer is wrong.

Try one more time.

Close your eyes.

Listen to the environment around you.

What do you feel?

Use all of your senses.

What do you see now?

I see my awakening.

I can see things that no longer serve me.

I can see a more poetic peaceful version of myself.

I am awakened.

Strength Within You

Lay upon gentle grass constellations morphed to a bull, push and pull all of the strength in *you*.

Outro: Healer

Its branches embrace your inner child with radiance and care.

Roots shuffle in the soil to soak all of your tears.

Pieces of tree bark represent your resilience to heal.

Remember to be patient—feeling stagnant is real. Birds chirp to your vibrant energy—sweeping you off your feet.

A peek of white light enters, as it reminds you of candy and sweets.

Hurts to cry—hurts to grow—hurts to reinvent yourself. This is what I know.

Your Heart froze all of your emotions in the snow.

The courageousness you exude is heavenly,

Never let it out of your sight. At the end of the tunnel, you are guaranteed to see the light.

ABOUT THE AUTHOR

Tai Timmerman, a poet and writer hailing from Brooklyn, New York, brings a unique blend of introspection and empathy to her work. As the author of "The Howling Wolf," "Commitment," "Anatomy of Our Friendship," and "Aristotle's Act of Virtue" in Empyrean Literary Magazine Issue 5: Vol 2, No 1, Tai delves deep into the complexities of the human experience.

Currently a Junior Biology major and Chemistry minor at Howard University, Tai's aspirations extend far beyond the classroom. With roots in Guyanese heritage and a drive to make a difference, she dreams of becoming a cardiovascular surgeon, dedicated to serving underserved communities.

In addition to her academic pursuits, Tai serves as a volunteer crisis counselor for Crisis Text Line, a Not for Profit Organization. It is this commitment to helping others, coupled with her own personal journey, that inspired her latest work, "I've Got Your Back." This collection of poetry offers a poignant exploration of mental health struggles and healing interventions, aiming to destigmatize and uplift those in need. Through her writing and crisis counseling, Tai seeks to make a meaningful impact, one heart and mind at a time.

www.ingramcontent.com/pod-product-compliance
Lightning Source LLC
LaVergne TN
LVHW052300100826
845147LV00001B/97

* 9 7 8 1 9 6 4 6 2 9 0 3 2 *